A Handbook For Adjunct and Part-Time Faculty

Donald Greive, Ed.D.

INFO-TEC, Inc. • Cleveland, Ohio

To Order:

INFO-TEC, Inc.
P.O. Box 40092
Cleveland, Ohio 44140
(216) 835-1610

LB
2 33/
67 2
198 4

Seventh Printing, October 1987

PREFACE

With the constant increase in the utilization of part-time faculty in higher education, it has become more and more evident that their development is an integral part of the success of many institutions. Unfortunately, the cost of in-service training for the large number of these individuals is prohibitive to most colleges and universities. Adjunct faculty members usually come to college teaching ranks with competence in their area of expertise but deficient in the professional skills necessary for the classroom.

This publication is intended to help remedy that situation. *A Handbook for Adjunct and Part-time Faculty* is written at the practioner's level emphasizing techniques and strategies adjunct faculty members may utilize. Although this publication is protected by copyright it is the intent of the author that faculty members receive the greatest support possible from its contents. Therefore faculty is granted permission to reproduce for personal use any of the forms in the publication that have direct application to their teaching.

CONTENTS

ABOUT THE AUTHOR

Donald Greive has spent the major portion of a professional career in higher education involved with part-time and adjunct faculty. During the 1960's and the student enrollment boom, he was involved in staffing classes with highly skilled part-time professionals and experts to help meet the educational needs of a booming American economy. He observed this trend continue until many institutions employed more part-time than full-time faculty. Later Dr. Greive spent over a decade administering and working with part-time faculty in the role of Director of Continuing Education and Evening Programs and Dean of Academic and Instructional Services. He has served as an adjunct faculty member at a state university, private liberal arts college, a technical institute and a community college. He and several associates previously authored *Teaching in College — A Resource for Adjunct and Part-Time Faculty*. He has managed several national conferences on the topic of adjunct and part-time faculty.

1

Teaching — What It's All About

A commonly accepted axiom in education is that learning is best accomplished when there is a need for the learning and when it is built upon former learning and knowledge. From these observations we can conclude that most learning, contrary to popular belief, is not the responsibility of teachers, but of learners. Faculty, as facilitators, however, can utilize the above principles to ease the learning tasks of students. The ideal situation, of course, is one in which both the need and former knowledge are in proper perspective.

Although learning starts with the knowledge and skills that students bring with them to class and not necessarily the content knowledge brought by faculty, teaching is still a vocation; a calling if you will, to individuals who enjoy being with people and feel intrinsic satisfaction in helping others and themselves to grow. Like parents, some teachers are better than others. Many people believe that teachers are born and not made. However, like parenting, many of the skills can be learned. With effort, personal dedication and sincerity, one can become an effective and good teacher.

Characteristics of Good Teaching

Using one's mind in the pursuit of knowledge and at the same time sharing with fellow citizens is in itself gratifying. The responsibility of a class and influence upon students is very stimulating. It remains stimulating, however, only so long as the teacher continues to grow and remain dynamic. We have all experienced mediocre performances by instructors. These performances were the responsibility of faculty who at one time were probably quite dynamic, but allowed themselves to slip into a rut. Whether one is just beginning to teach or is an experienced instructor, one must constantly strive to avoid that situation.

The qualities of good teaching are quite simple:

- *Knowing one's subject content*
- *Knowing and liking the students*
- *Understanding one's culture in general*

Knowing One's Subject Content. Faculty cannot assume that they will be accepted as experts by students simply because they are in front of the class. Students are quick to question faculty members' competence if errors are committed. With technology changing so rapidly and students of all ages exposed to the opportunity to obtain new information about a variety of subjects, faculty need to constantly remain alert to information and developments within their discipline or field of study.

Knowing and Liking Students. Adjunct faculty members must expect students of varying abilities and backgrounds. Students seeking knowledge and competencies as well as students seeking only social opportunities will be present in the classroom. Modern faculty can ill afford to "expect" certain types of students to enroll in their classes. The bottom line to success in working with the diverse student body is to: *work at it; view students as people, not clients; be flexible in setting rules; and above all be fair.*

Understanding One's Culture and Life in General. This topic is, of course, too broad to discuss in detail here. As was indicated earlier, student expectations of faculty are significant. Faculty must stay abreast of events outside of their discipline. News, entertainment, sports events, cultural events or significant scientific developments outside of one's field will often serve to open avenues of communication with students and establish one's credibility. Most of us are familiar with college instructors with tunnel vision and remember the low esteem in which they were held. The writer recalls that while enrolled as an undergraduate in an advanced mathematics course (during a presidential election year and after considerable comment by the instructor on the importance of taking part in the democratic process) the faculty member scheduled a major examination the morning following the election despite the fact that televised election returns were then new and watched by all very late the previous night. Knowledge of activities outside one's own discipline and flexibility are necessary to good teaching.

The First Class — The Size Up

As a beginning faculty member approaches his/her first class, considerable anxiety and nervousness will be experienced. This has always been true of teaching and will continue to be true in the future. In fact, many experienced teachers feel they do their best work if they are slightly nervous and anxious. Excessive nervousness and anxiety, however, can be a distraction into the teaching-learning process and efforts should be made to minimize them.

In preparation for the first class one must keep in mind that it is nearly impossible to completely prepare for any class. The speed at which the class presentation will go usually cannot be anticipated. Many times student response is significantly greater or less than expected. *Having excessive material prepared for the first class, as well as all classes, is worth the extra effort in confidence gained.*

Another major factor in facing the first class is to *know yourself as a teacher.* Anyone mature enough to be teaching has some feeling of their own personal characteristics. Most of us are average in appearance, however, we usually have gone through life compensating for variations from the average. There is no more need to be self-conscious of personal appearance in front of a class than there is in any social situation. Minor compensations, however, may be necessary. If one has a tendency toward casual or even sloppy appearance, appearing neat and professional will pay off. If one has an untrained or light voice, practice in expression may be well worth the time spent. If one is especially charming or handsome, concentration on teaching and not impressing the class may be necessary. Generally speaking, part of the student size up will include the appearance and actions of the teacher. Being in control pays off in not only eliminating barriers to classroom communication, but in developing self-confidence in teaching.

Remember, students usually are not solely impressed by the knowledge and experience of the teacher, they are equally influenced by related factors. Many adjunct faculty members have lost their class the first night simply because they assumed the students were there to share their pearls of wisdom, when in fact the students were "sizing up" the teacher.

Some guidelines for the first class are as follows:

- Be over-prepared rather than under-prepared.

- Plan an activity that allows students to get involved immediately. This may simply be an information gathering format.

- Initiate casual conversation between yourself and students and among the students prior to launching into the specifics of the course.

- Be aware of over-preparation of subject matter that may leave one under-prepared for the class. Find out ahead of time the number of students expected, previous course requirements, etc.

- Don't rely on tips from experienced teachers; they are coming from a different perspective and are different individuals.

- Conduct a class — don't meet and dismiss. First impressions are most lasting.

Adjunct faculty should not hesitate at the beginning of the first class to share their background and experiences with students. It is not necessary to brag or be modest. However, many students are distracted trying to "psych out" or "figure out" the faculty member. Teachers should tell their background, professional preparation and why they are there. In turn, students should not be asked for more information than the teacher has given about him/herself.

Effective implementation of the previously outlined first class strategies is important. Listed below are some tips:

1. Immediate communication can be established by oral communication initiated by the faculty member. Don't hesitate to use small talk, information about yourself or general comments concerning the course.

2. The first activity should be physical in nature. It is very important to commence interaction with class. Asking for a show of hands of students with previous work, holding up the textbook to identify it; having students introduce themselves or write comments concerning their reason for being there are some techniques. Giving adequate time for students' questions is also quite important.

3. Make a specific assignment for the next class session and supply appropriate background for the course.

Setting The Tone

Professional educators and teacher trainers agree that the greatest task in teaching is to motivate students to feel good about the course in which they are enrolled. Creating positive feelings about the course is the responsibility of the teacher. Even though students may be taking courses outside their major area, it is possible to promote a good feeling if appropriate positive activities are introduced. Teachers, through their appearance, actions and personality, can be very influential in the development of those feelings.

In setting the tone of the classroom, faculty often overlook a very basic human trait. Very often they assume the students are aware of the fact that they intend to be pleasant, cooperative and helpful. This cannot be taken for granted. With differing personalities and types of students that are in the classroom, faculty members must realize that a positive comment or gesture to one student may in fact be negative to another student. Thus, faculty should make a concerted effort to show their pleasantness by their behavior. The smile, a pleasant comment or a laugh with students who are attempting to be funny will pay great dividends. Even setting little cues for oneself is helpful. The author, in the presentation of a workshop that he conducts and has a tendency occasionally to get too serious, leaves a sign on the podium facing only himself with the simple words "be pleasant." It is amazing the number of times one must be reminded.

It is also important to realize in setting the tone of the classroom that permissiveness is not always bad. We are all familiar with traditional teaching in which students were expected to remain quiet and "stay in their place." We are also familiar with situations where excessive permissiveness was allowed that was a distraction to other students. College teachers must be cognizant of the fact that flexibility and permissiveness are a necessity in a proper learning atmosphere and that encouraging creativity and unexpected comments is part of the learning and teaching process. Excessive distraction, due to flexibility, can always be controlled by the faculty member because he/she is the authority in the room. The instructor has ultimate authority, and need not exercise it to prove it for its own sake. Remember permissiveness and flexibility requires considerable working skill. Authority is there with the role.

Teachers are Actors/Actresses

In reality, faculty members are on stage; they are actors or actresses whether or not they admit and recognize it. A teacher in front of the classroom carries all of the responsibility and requires all of the talent of anyone on stage or taking part in a performance. Due to modern technology, unfortunately, students compare faculty to professionals they have seen in other roles. Thus, adjunct faculty must be alert to the ramifications.

Faculty members have within themselves all of the emotions of stage performers with greater interacting with the audience. There may be, on occasion, an emotional reaction and one must be equipped to deal with it. As an instructor, one will experience fear, joy, feelings of tentativeness, and feelings of extreme confidence and satisfaction. Handle fear with good *preparation;* confidence brought forward with good preparation is the easiest way to ally fear. Remove anxieties from the classroom by developing communication systems. Some adjunct faculty members are effective at using humor. As a general rule, however, humor must be used delicately. *Jokes are completely out.* Almost any joke that is told in the classroom will offend someone. Another caution, *don't let compassion become sympathy for students.* As a faculty member you cannot handle your students' family, career and personal problems. And finally, *it is not necessary to exert or exercise authority.* You already possess such authority and will call upon it when needed.

Student Characteristics

Although much has been written in recent years concerning social strata, it is impossible to categorize students in terms of social characteristics. In fact, an attempt to do so is dangerous and teachers should strive to avoid any implications of stereotyping. There are, however, expectations on the part of the students that probably were not evident until recently. According to Burrill (Greive, *et al.,* 1983) these expectations fall into six categories.

1. *Today's students are much more self-directed than their earlier counterparts.*

   Adult students many times are working full-time or are full-time housewives coming back to the classroom. They are generally highly self-directed in terms of their objectives. They will, and have been, involved probably in hundreds of hours of educational endeavors outside of the classroom, many times to learn something new. They can easily be put down and become frustrated if spoon fed with information that is designed for high school students.

2. *Today's students are highly demanding as consumers.*

   Adults, in contrast to college age students, are paying for their education. They want their money's worth. They have high expectations for learning something worthwhile and hold the teacher responsible. Many times they will audibly resent time being wasted in class on trivial, irrelevant and unimportant issues. They may even become hostile if they sense their money is being wasted.

3. *Today's students very often come to the classroom with rich life experiences.*

   They frequently are able to understand and have read about theoretical concepts that in the past were not thought of. They have the ability to relate these concepts to their own experiences. They generally like to share these experiences which can be an asset to the classroom if it is relevant to the content, but can be an interference if it is not related to the classroom objectives.

4. *Today's new students will demand that they be treated as adults.*

They expect to be addressed as peers, respected as mature individuals. They perceive themselves to be equal and conceivable professionally superior to the teacher. They will react immediately with hostility to condescending attitudes.

5. *Today's students will demand relevance and immediate application.*

   In contrast to the 1960s relevance had best be associated with career or life advancement rather than social ideals. Today's students have a strong need to use the information immediately and be able to see how the information relates to a particular situation. They will question and test the relevance of concepts and thoughts and are demanding outgoing consumers.

6. *The new students may demand a part in developing the learning activity.*

   They will not tolerate passivity and will not sit idly by and watch what is going on. They will expect participation, sharing and achievement and they expect to do something on behalf of their own learning and education.

In summary, the characteristics of students, whom we find in the classroom today, demand a thorough review of your teaching methodology. Reading from the old yellow note pad will no longer satisfy today's students.

Aggressive Students

One of the greatest fears for beginning and experienced faculty is the possibility of encountering a consistently aggressive and argumentative student. This type of student can, if allowed, dominate the class and make it uncomfortable as well as waste the valuable time of other students. Although generally these problems are minimized if the teacher continues in a businesslike fashion, occasionally, a persistent student will become a problem. Teachers in this situation can attempt a variety of time proven strategies.

They are reviewed here only as suggestions and not as a panacea.

Communicating verbally to the aggressive student is best done if eye contact is maintained. In fact, many times direct eye contact without direct response is sufficient to deliver the message. Use of humor with an upset student is dangerous. The use of light humor on a disassociated topic may, however, reduce the tension in a stressful situation. Asking students to state their problem very often will clarify the situation. Of course, the verbal request for the student to stop for a conference after class is very often effective — keeping in mind that the real problem is probably not the issue being verbalized in class, but some underlying issue. Above all, teachers should examine their own behavior. Are they doing something or inferring something that is irritating to one or more students? Finally, a strategy that is very seldom necessary is simply to indicate to the student in a dire situation that no more class time can be taken on the issue and that if his sole purpose in class is to discuss the issue then he is wasting his time and the time of the other students. A faculty member must be cautious not to intimidate the student or "put them down," not to argue with the student and to keep his cool — when teachers lose their cool they are no longer in command.

Student Types

Since historically adult students are the newest clientele, there has been little effective research published concerning the learning styles of adult students. It is known, however, that adult students have a high social need as they enter college for the first time or for the first time after an extended absence. This characteristic may change later as they become more comfortable and their aspirations switch to a higher degree of achievement. According to Kazmierski (Greive, *et al.*, 1983), in the average classroom there are essentially six types of learners. They are:

1. *The preceptive, intuitive.*
   These individuals gather information discriminately and

categorically but evaluate it by intuition. The typical classroom behavior of these people would probably include a high facility for knowledgeable discussions in the class, but may result in drawing inappropriate conclusions for written or test work, thus, the teacher must be aware that although these students will achieve well in the content area of multiple choice or essay questions, they may have their own opinions in terms of the analysis which may or may not be the teacher's expectations.

2. *The reflective, systematic students.*

These students will take in random and extensive information, but evaluate it in a systematic way. These students will reach conclusions based upon hard data they have developed. The possible error in working with these students is the fact that some of the random and extensive information they have gathered may not be as their interpretation would indicate. It is quite difficult in discussing issues with these students to convince them, that another position might be considered. In their mind they have collected all of the data available.

3. *The preceptive, systematic student.*

Preceptive, systematic students are characterized by limited, but categorized information gathering with regular systematic evaluations. Probably these students and the resultant graduate is best described by the old saying, "statistics don't lie, but statisticians do." Obviously, the danger encountered by these students is that all statistics or information are not gathered before their evaluation is made. We are all aware of biases in sampling and resultant conclusions. Statisticians are people of a preceptive, systematic mode. Although they may admit there is a probability factor that their conclusions are wrong, they will defend to the end their process and the conclusions they reached based upon their evaluations.

4. *Receptive-intuitive.*
Receptive, intuitive students tend to be the more artistic students. Every class has a few of these students. They are the students who do not seem to fit in the structured mode of the class and always raise the unexpected question. Usually the questions are intelligent, not silly and are thought provoking. Appropriate utilization of these students can be very effective in adding to class discussion and interest. These students gather extensive data but will not usually have all the facts together before they raise issues or reach conclusions. They are truly the creative individuals in our society.

5. *Exclusive information gatherers.*
These individuals are concerned only about data. They will have information and data on many facts and may go to extended efforts to get information concerning an issue or a point which may or may not relate to the objectives of the course. They will then have difficulty understanding why their contribution is not important. Again, appropriately prepared course objectives clearly communicated can minimize the problems produced by these students. Very rarely do these individuals take time to evaluate the information they have gathered. Many of society's trivia collectors fit into this category. They can add interesting anecdotes to the class but they are a danger if allowed to dominate the class.

6. *Exclusive evaluation specialists.*
These are the individuals who are not particularly concerned with information as it relates to a profession. Many of these people are "risers." Individuals who rise to the top due to political savvy, friends, but not necessarily from information, knowledge or competence. They love to

spend their talents making decisions on information that others have brought in. Teachers may recognize these individuals as the "apple polishers" of the class.

Classroom Communication

Many kinds of communication exist in every classroom situation. Faculty must be aware that the expression on their face, their eye contact with students, as well as students' interacting is constantly going on regardless of the intentions.

The major concern of teachers is that this communication be structured as a positive learning situation.

Communication starts the moment the instructor steps into the classroom on the first day or evening of class. As is indicated elsewhere in this publication, the method, by which faculty introduce themselves and the initial interaction with students, is indicative to students of the type of communication that will exist throughout the course. The amount of student participation as the course progresses is an indicator of the direction in which the communication is flowing. It can easily be determined by tape recording a class and later recording the time the instructor talks versus the time the students respond.

A whole new field of body language, of which there is a significant amount of recent literature, is probably worth pursuing for beginning faculty. Beginning faculty should be certain to control habitual gestures that to them are automatic, but to students may be distractive.

Gestures. Most non-verbal gestures are well-known to faculty and students. For example, it is known that eye contact, or lack of same, indicates many things. Casual eye contact will indicate disinterest or lack of attention or possibly even lack of understanding of the discussion. Extended eye contact may signal aggression or resentment on the part of the students. Effective and timely eye contact can reduce psychological differences between individuals and faculty. Remember, analysis of eye contact with the class can indicate to the instructor if communication channels are open or closed.

Gestures or movements of parts of the body are other ways of non-verbal communication. Obviously, the age old concept of pointing the finger by the teacher means "pay attention to the point." In addition to the pointing of the finger, keep in mind that generally in our culture making a point with the hand extended palm up is a positive and supportive gesture, whereas a downward direction of the palm indicates a negative reaction. Students are very conscious of gestures. Simply walking back and forth in front of a class, if it is not nervous pacing, indicates an interest in the environment in which one is working. Using the hands and arms to demonstrate space or extended distance is effective. Gestures can be instructional, supportive and effective or they can be distracting. Faculty should make every effort to determine which of the gestures are adding to the instructional process and which are personal mannerisms that may be distracting.

Another non-verbal activity that is often used and must be highly controlled is facial expression. Facial expression is somewhat automatic in reaction to a response. Teachers, if they are not careful, may reflect dissatisfaction or lack of acceptance to a student response when it was not intended. On the other hand, appropriate use of facial expressions can indicate approval and consideration for thoughts and response even though they may not be accurate.

When facing the class, posture is also important. Leaning toward the class or walking toward it indicates acceptance and generally liking the situation. Obviously, the reverse is also true.

The Three R's

Much has been written about the three R's of learning. The author, however, feels that the three R's of teaching are equally important. Good communication in the classroom, which the teacher controls, is necessary for successful teaching learning situation. The three R's of good teaching are: *repeat, respond and reinforce.* Very simply they mean: student comments and contributions, if worthy of being recognized in class, are worthy of being repeated. A simple repetitious repeat, however, is not sufficient. One should elicit an additional response either from the class, or the student making the original statement. After the response is obtained, reinforcement of the statement or conclusions should be stated. These three simple rules do many things to improve class relationships. They emphasize the importance of the student, students to each other, and what they say. It promotes two way communication and applies one of the basic tenants of learning: *reinforcement.*

Checklist for Part-Time Faculty

There are an undetermined number of things that part-time faculty need to know. Each teaching situation may elicit new information necessary. There are, however, basic items that part-time faculty should know and almost assuredly will be asked at some time during class. This section lists items that a faculty member may wish to check over before entering the first class.

FACULTY CHECK LIST

1. When are grades due? When do students receive grades?

2. Is there a college or departmental grading policy?

3. Is there a departmental course syllabus, course outline or statement of goals and objectives available for the course?

4. Are there prepared departmental handouts?

5. Are there prepared departmental tests?

6. What is the library book checkout procedure?

7. What instructional support aids are available?

8. What are the bookstore policies?

9. Is there a department and/or college attendance or tardiness policy?

10. Where is and how do I get my copy of the text and supportive materials for teaching the class?

11. Where can I get instructional aid materials, films, video tapes, etc., and what is the lead time for ordering?

12. What is the name of the department chairperson? Dean, other college officials?

13. Have I completed all of my paperwork for official employment (an expected paycheck that doesn't arrive is demoralizing).

2

Planning

There are many suggestions for good teaching discussed in this publication, however, the most important activity for faculty is planning for their teaching. With the rising expectations of students, faculty who do not adequately plan will have a difficult time being effective and respected. Basically, planning for teaching is giving direction and reason to the course and the teaching of the course. We have all heard in some form or another the old saying, "it doesn't make any difference which direction you go if you don't know where you're going." Translated, this simply means that if one does not plan adequately it will not make any difference how good a teacher he/she is, one will not be effective.

As students, observing our past professors, we sometimes felt that planning consisted of getting ready for next week or the next class. Often in undergraduate classes we were faced with the problem that with two weeks to go in the term, there were still four or five weeks of material to cover because the professor had digressed too often from the objectives of the course. This practice is unfair to students who are expected to have achieved certain competencies before moving onto a higher level of study. Faculty should view planning in the initial stages as a reverse process. *Looking at one's destination and then developing a plan to reach the destination is a sound and effective practice.*

The Lesson Plan

The lesson plan should be used as a reference and not as a fixed guide. It should have a definite purpose, indicating the main thoughts for the lesson; it should be numbered and arranged as part of a total plan for the course. The lesson plan should be flexible to allow discussion of current events when it is appropriate. The lesson plan should be developed in such a way that if media or support activities are needed, a backup system is available in event the materials do not arrive, or there is a mechanical or electrical defect. The plan should contain key questions and quotes from supplemental material not contained in the text. Lesson plans should include definitions, comments on purposes of the class, student activities and teacher activities.

Faculty should make every effort to make lesson plans reflect their creative endeavors and their unique ability as teachers. Often, the syllabus and to some extent the course outline are dictated to teachers. The demands for accountability and the goals of the institution constrict these two documents and limit their flexibility. Lesson plans, however, allow the greatest opportunity for flexibility and permit unique techniques. The lesson plan is a unique opportunity to prove to oneself how good one really is. Shown in figures 1 and 2 are examples of a lesson plan and a sample form. *An effective method of planning a course is to construct at least one of these plans for each day the class meets, appropriately number them, place them in a loose leaf binder and maintain them as a record and a guide for activities.*

Figure 1

Sample Lesson Plan

Course # and Name: Algebra 101

Date _____

Session # *9*

Definitions:

1. Equation is statement that two expressions are equal.
2. Expression is a mathematical statement.
3. Linear equation is equation of 1st order.

Class Objectives:

1. To demonstrate equations through use of various expressions of equality.
2. To prove equality of expressions through technique of substitutions.

Student Activities:

1. Complete sample problems in class.
2. Demonstrate competence of sample by board work.

Instructor Activities:

1. Demonstrate validity of solutions of equations.
2. Assure student understanding by personal observations by seat and board work.
3. Give non-graded quiz over basic equations.

Major Impact:

1. Understanding of appreciation of solution of basic linear equations.

Assignment: Problems — Exercise 8, pp. 41-42.

Figure 2

Suggested Lesson Plan Format

Course number and name
(after first page simply number chronologically)

Date _____

Session # _____

Definitions to be covered _____

_____

Class Objective(s) _____

_____

Student activities or exercises _____

_____

Instructor activities _____

_____

Major impact or thought _____

_____

Assignment _____

_____

The Course Outline

While the lesson plan is a daily map for teachers to ensure their direction and activity for a given session, the course outline is much more comprehensive and allows faculty to monitor the map of the entire course. Course outlines allow faculty in a structured format to add and include their personal and professional anecdotes as they relate to the class topics.

The course outline is usually a formal document. A standard outline form will usually suffice to cover in detail the topics to be addressed. Generally, a topic need not be divided into more than three subtopics for a class outline. Detail more significant than three subtopics should be placed in the daily class lesson plan. *The purpose of the outline is very simple: to make certain that all major topics are recognized and addressed during the course.*

The two types of outlines most commonly used in teaching are the *chronological outline and the content outline.* Content outlines are used with topics to be covered in a specified content order. It is often called a topical outline. The chronological outline is self-descriptive. Courses which lend themselves to time and historic development lend themselves to a chronological outline. Even sequential courses, such as mathematics and science, where previous knowledge is necessary to function at a higher level, are considered chronological outlines. Content outlines allow considerable flexibility. They allow faculty to arrange the content of the course in a way that is most effective for presentation. For example, physical education faculty may allow students to actually take part in an activity prior to teaching some of the basic fundamentals, so that the students can see a need for the techniques. Whereas a chronological outline would call for the presentation of the basic information, before an attempt to perform is undertaken. If one is teaching a course concerned with legislative, judicial or community activities, it is not absolutely necessary that field trips to legislative bodies, court rooms, etc., be conducted in sequence with other activities in the course.

Although in most institutions there are course outlines available, generally they will not be filed and maintained as formal documents. Often they are treated in the same manner as lesson plans, to be developed by the instructor. The formal document recognized at most institutions and approved by the college is the course syllabus. A sample of a course outline is shown in figure 3. Theoretically, a proper course outline is developed in direct relation to the objectives written for the course. This assures direction and purpose of the outline.

Figure 3

Sample Course Outline
Statistics

I. INTRODUCTION
  A. Basic Statistics
  1. Purposes
  B. Data Gathering
  1. Samples
    a. Instruments
  2. Recorded Data
    a. Machine utilization

II. PRESENTING DATA
  A. Tables
  1. Summary Tables
    a. Table Elements
    b. Tables with averages
  B. Graphs
  1. Types of Graphs
    a. Bar
    b. Pi chart
    c. Line graph
  2. Data Presentation with Graphs
  C. Frequency Distributions
  1. Discrete and Continuous
  2. Class Interval

III. DESCRIPTION AND COMPARISON OF
DISTRIBUTIONS
  A. Percentiles
  1. Computation of percentile
  2. Inter Percentile Range
  3. Percentile Score
  B. Mean and Standard Deviations
  1. Computation of Mean

        a. From grouped data
        b. From arbitrary origin
    2. Variance formulas
  C. Frequency Distributions
    1. Measures of central tendency
    2. Symmetry & skewness
    3. Pi modal distributions

IV. PREDICTIVE OR ESTIMATIVE TECHNIQUES
  A. Regression
    1. Computation for regression formula
    2. Application of formula
        a. Graphic
        b. Assumptions of linearity
  B. Correlation
    1. Computation of Correlation Coefficient
        a. Reliability of measurement
  C. Circumstances affecting regression and analysis
    1. Errors of measurement
    2. Effect or range
    3. Interpretation of size

V. THE NORMAL CURVE AND STATISTICAL INFERENCE
  A. The Normal Distribution
    1. Mean
    2. Standard Deviation
    3. Characteristics
  B. Statistical Inference
    1. Employing samples
        a. Randomness
        b. Parameters
    2. Normal Distribution
        a. Standard Error
        b. Unbiased Estimate
        c. Confidence Interval

C. Testing Hypothesis
  1. Definition of Statistical Hypothesis
  2. Test of Hypothesis
    a. Level of Significance
    b. One Sided Test
  3. Computing Power of Test

The Course Syllabus

A syllabus is defined as "a concise statement of the main points of a course of study or subject." Although this definition leaves room for interpretation (for example, what constitutes concise? and what constitutes the main points?), one thing is certain: the syllabus is the official document of the course. The syllabus is the document that should be shared with students, filed as a permanent contribution to the instructional archives of the campus and is the legal document in the event litigation may arise due to student complaints or concerns. Thus, it is probably the most important document in the educational process.

The reason there is considerable confusion in academia concerning syllabi is that faculty members may interpret the definition of a syllabus differently. For example, a concise statement to one faculty member may simply mean the words "Chapter V"; whereas to another faculty member it may mean enumerating the major points of Chapter V; describing them and writing a complete sentence concerning each. Even though the syllabus is deemed one of the most important documents in education, part-time faculty probably will encounter situations where such a document is not available. There are two reasons for this:

  1. Course development and presentation have been left completely to the wishes of individual faculty members and they are not required to make it available to institutional sources.

2. Part-time faculty members may be teaching a new or recently revised course for which a syllabus has not been developed.

There are situations where part-time faculty will be called upon to develop a syllabus for their own course.

Development of the syllabus is a multi-step process. A good syllabus has several major parts. They are:

1. The complete name of the course, including the course number.
2. The name and title by which the faculty member wishes to be addressed.
3. The faculty member's office hours.
4. The text or texts and outside readings required.
5. The course requirements and grading standards.
6. The course objectives.
7. The assignments, projects, etc., to be completed by the students.
8. A complete listing of resources, outside readings, field trips, etc.

Objectives. The first major part of the syllabus is the listing of the course objectives. Listing the objectives for a course often is difficult for new faculty members. The tendency is to make certain that everything of importance in the course is listed. This dilutes the purpose of the objectives and makes them less valuable to the teaching process. As a general rule, most courses can be adequately described by the listing of not more than ten to fourteen objectives. One must be certain, however, that the objectives are reachable, they are teachable, and student learning activities can be directed to each.

Student Activities. Following the objectives should be a section that describes the activities of the students that result in their meeting the objectives of the course. This should include in some detail specific activities such as: outside reading, laboratory activities, projects, assignments, etc. It is best to describe these activities in a way that they relate directly to objectives. Significant attention should be given to the reasons for the activities and how they relate to the course. This approach conveys to the students the impression that the class is all business and that there is a purpose for everything. It is also helpful to share with the students the activities in which the faculty member plans to be involved.

Course Requirements. Next the syllabus should include a detailed description of the course requirements and the expectations of students in terms of handing in assignments, tests, quizzes and the procedure that will be used in the evaluation of the student. This is one of the most important parts of the syllabus because it defines for students exactly what is expected and eliminates the possibility at a later date to claim ignorance of what was expected. In fact, it is useful in this section of the syllabus to list the class meetings by day and date, the specific reading and homework assignments expected and other activities and class topics to be achieved at that time. Many experienced faculty members have felt that all this detail was not necessary until they found themselves in an indefensible position concerning student accusations that the course content was not adequately covered. Sometimes this section of the syllabus is broken into two or more parts, however, the general rule is that excessive detail is better than too little detail.

Resources and References. Finally, the syllabus should include a complete listing of resources, outside readings, bibliographies, visitations, etc., to which the student may wish to refer. Without fail, required outside readings and library reserve assignments should be specified. Again, excessive detail is of value. One need not be concerned if the syllabus eventually grows into a document of five or six pages. The students, in the long run, will be appreciative of the faculty member's efforts and the instructor will be adequately protected in the event evidence of course content or teacher preparation is needed.

The syllabus should be distributed to the students the first day of class. Time should be taken to discuss the syllabus and details therein. In fact, it is good practice to go over the syllabus the second meeting of the class. It would be well to describe in detail the activities expected of students as they relate to certain assignments and objectives. A good syllabus requires considerable work initially and considerable time in subsequent updates. Work put into the development of the syllabus will pay dividends. *A syllabus is a scientific document and a work of art and it should be shown that respect in its development and use.*

Figure 4 is a sample of a completed syllabus.

Figure 4

Achievement University
Syllabus

Name of Course:
> History 200

Faculty Name:
> Dr. Madeline Jones — Dr. Jones

Office Hours:
> MWF, 8:00-9:00 a.m., 2:00-3:00 p.m.
> TR, 1:00-2:00 p.m.

Text:
> (Author, Name, Edition, publisher)

Course Requirements:
> Outside readings (general and reserved list, projects) (specify, clarify, including due dates project list attached, etc.)

Grading:
> Midterm — essay, 30% of final grade
> Final — multiple choice, 30% of final grade

Class project and class participation (including quizzes)
40% of final grade

Class Objectives:

1. To enumerate the events, attitudes, economic chances, innovations that lead to economic growth during antebellum era.

2. To describe the effect on social, political, philosophical life, and the nation's economic structure due to the growth and development during the antebellum era.

3. To interpret the meaning of Jacksonian democracy of the different social economic groups in the American society.

4. To enumerate the factors that lead to Andrew Jackson being viewed as a popular hero and tyrannical president and an agent of special interest groups.

5. To describe the impact of political groups of Jacksonian democracy.

6. To enumerate the moral and social causes, other than abolishionism in antebellum America.

7. To describe the European influence on American culture in terms of economic expansion, frontier experience and political and social reform during the antebellum era.

8. To describe the roots including economic, political, social, demographic and diplomatic factors that lead to American expansionism in the 1840's.

9. To describe the many different economic, ideological, political and social factors that lead to the Civil War.

10. To describe several issues related to slavery that went beyond the morality of bondage.

11. To describe the effect the Civil War had on America's economy and politics.

12. To enumerate the circumstances leading to the North's victory in the Civil War.

13. To enumerate the reasons why the radical reconstruction failed after the Civil War.

Student Exercises:

Completion of all examinations, quizzes and projects listed under requirements. The completion of the reading of texts, specific assignments by class session listed, and outside readings as assigned. Submission of an 8 page topic paper (insert date) selected from a list of topics distributed in the class.

Resources Reading:

(Listing of text, outside readings, reserved materials, special reference materials and personal resources outside of the classroom.)

Writing Objectives

Whether one adopts the structures described in the previous paragraphs or decides to utilize a combination of the previous outlines in addition to their own creative endeavors, sooner or later it is realized that objectives for the students must be written. The educational scene a few years ago was literally attacked with "objective fever." The writer recalls while working on doctoral level studies that some educational psychologists seemed "possessed" with the use of the proper word, be it adjective or noun, in order to construct a "proper" objective. This coming after several years of graduate and undergraduate study where professors failed to develop the premise of preparing objectives at all, indeed, showed an evolutionary concept in education. Fortunately, at the present time neither of these extremes exists. It is known by most practioners that objectives can be written in many forms and can even be communicated verbally and learning will still take place. The format in which the objectives are written is not as important as it was once thought.

The basis for modern objective writing is a taxonomy of educational objectives developed by Benjamin Bloom (Bloom, 1956). Bloom states that learning takes place in three domains. They are:

a. The cognitive

b. The affective

c. The psychomotor

Cognitive. The cognitive domain is that which most instructors think of as intellectual learning. This domain includes the mental development of the individual. The levels of learning at the cognitive domain include:

1. Knowledge

2. Comprehension

3. Application

4. Analysis

5. Synthesis

6. Evaluation

An analysis of the cognitive domain is shown in Figure 5.

Figure 5

Cognitive Domain

Level	Student Activity
Knowledge	Recall — Memorize
Comprehensive	Understand — Translate
Application	Apply — Related Activities
Analysis	Actualize Parts & whole
Synthesis	Utilize Uniquely
Evaluation	Make Judgment

Affective. The affective domain concerns students' values and to some degree their emotions. The affective domain is the most difficult to relate to an instructional situation. Students often have difficulty learning due to past values or emotional concerns. Faculty must be constantly alert to the fact that the affective domain may have significant effect upon the teaching/learning process, but is most difficult to prepare for.

Psychomotor. The psychomotor domain emphasizes motor skills or physical activity. This domain applies to those classes where physical skills are necessary. Faculty in physical education or other courses utilizing equipment rely heavily on this domain.

When writing objectives for the class, faculty should attempt to write objectives that cover all three domains. It is easy for instructors to fall into the practice of writing primarily knowledge level objectives in the cognitive domain. When the class is developed around the cognitive domain, students who can quickly memorize and respond achieve a high grade, whereas students with analysis or synthesis skills are not challenged to their capabilities.

Robert Mager, one of the pioneers of the instructional objectives movement, outlines several principles not observed in writing objectives (Mager, 1962). Mager states that effective instructional objectives must:

a. Be explicit

b. Communicate

c. Tell what the learner will be doing

d. Indicate conditions to be imposed

e. Include some recognition of whether or not it was achieved

Being explicit means that the objective should say something about an activity and can be measured. General statements such as "to explain" or "to discuss" are not acceptable objective descriptors. For example, to know, to understand, to believe, to grasp are words that are open to interpretation according to Mager. On the other hand, to write, to identify, to differentiate, to solve, to construct, to list are examples of words that communicate clearly the expectation of the objective. Some objectives will contain conditions under which students are expected to perform. These conditions might include: given the formula for, given the solutions of, given the following quotations, from which students will then develop an outcome based upon those conditions.

The final elements that are included in writing objectives is the criteria for success. A typical criteria for success might be the time in which the person completes something, the number of pages described in the activity and the competency level obtained at the completion of the activity.

Examples of some objectives written to the previous criteria are shown below:

1. Given a list of linear equations, the student will find and test the appropriate solution at the 90 percent level of correctness within an hour.

2. The student will write a fifty word paragraph on one of the following topics (list several) using correct mechanics and form.

3. The student will show an appreciation of the theatre by voluntarily reading two selections from a list of outside plays provided to the class during the period of the course.

4. After five practice sessions, the student will be able to return the tennis ball, over the net, for a sustained period of four volleys.

Note that the first two objectives are in the cognitive domain, the third one is in the affective domain and the final is in the psychomotor domain.

Conclusion. If the reader at this time feels confused by the multitude of topics discussed in this chapter, he is reacting normally. Remember, John Dewey once stated that the first step in learning is confusion. The topics presented here are an analysis of topics that could be discussed in detail in complete publications in themselves. This is intended to provide adjunct faculty with the expertise necessary to develop their own teaching strategies. The most important component of teaching is the faculty member's preparation. Differing personalities, student attitudes, student types, content management, content knowledge, etc., are all important, but the most important criterion for successful teaching is good preparation.

If one is teaching a part-time class for the first time, one will not be adequately paid for the time spent in preparation. In order to face a class confidently and effectively each meeting, extensive preparation is needed.

The options presented here provide an avenue to do that preparation. Regardless of the method selected, faculty should adopt a system of preparation, perfect it to their own personality and style, and enter each class prepared to deliver a professional activity.

Faculty Self-Evaluation

Many colleges today have forms available for faculty who wish to conduct self-evaluations. If used, whether voluntary or mandatory, it must be kept in mind that most of these forms are in fact student opinionnaires, not statistically valid instruments. A disadvantage of such instruments is that they do not accurately reflect what has transpired in the class. Such generalized questions as "instructor's knowledge of subject matter" almost always appear on such documents, when in fact it is impossible for students to make such evaluations when they are not knowledgeable in the subject matter. Also, usually such forms are much too long and ask many irrelevant, detailed questions which infringe upon the validity of the instrument.

This does not, however, diminish the value of faculty seeking student input to improve their teaching. Whether one is an experienced faculty member or new to the profession, one will invariably find surprises while conducting such evaluations. New faculty members will be astonished at some of the observations students make. The writer recalls an experience with an acquaintance who was considered by his associates and himself to possess an effective sense of humor. However, after conducting a self-evaluation in the classroom, he was surprised to find that the students not only rated him low, but many felt he did not possess a sense of humor. (Whether or not the results of student sampling of this type precipitate a change in behavior of the faculty member is not important.) It is important, however, that faculty know how they are being perceived by the students.

There are two identifiable characteristics that are consistently valued by the students in relation to faculty behavior. They are:

1. Their businesslike behavior in the classroom.

2. Being understanding and friendly.

Figure 6 is an evaluation form that faculty members may use to conduct self-evaluation. Note that the form exists in three sections:

- Classroom evaluations

- Course related factors

- Teacher personal evaluation

This form may be reproduced in its entirety if desired, however, there probably will be a desire, especially in sections two and three of the evaluation form, to add class related questions.

The first section of the form (classroom evaluation) is an attempt to obtain insight concerning behavior in the classroom as it is viewed by the students. The second section of the evaluation form (course related factors) may vary considerably depending upon the type of course. Some courses lend themselves extensively to course related factors while other classes may not. The final section (teacher personal evaluation) gives the faculty member an opportunity to select some personal evaluation characteristics that they may wish to review occasionally. Questions may be added or deleted to this form at will.

It must be remembered that student perceptions are very often motivated by personal biases and problems rather than objective evaluation of the instructor. The continued use of a form of this type is helpful to faculty to determine if there are characteristics that continue to surface that need attention. Many statistical techniques can be applied to evaluation forms such as this. A simple method of utilizing the form is to ask the students to assign grades to each of these categories and then weigh them on a number scale. To fully utilize a flexible instrument such as this, extra weight can be given to factors that are deemed more important by the faculty member and less weight to those that are of less importance, in order to improve the validity of the responses. It is not intended that this self-evaluation form contain content validity; however, it should be comprehensive enough to give faculty members insight into their teaching situation.

Figure 6

Faculty Evaluation Form

CLASS: _____

DATE: _____

INSTRUCTIONS: Please grade each factor on a scale of A-F in terms of your perception of the teacher's behavior or characteristics.

Classroom Evaluation

Preparation for class   _____

Communication of classroom expectation to students   _____

Command of subject matter   _____

Professional and businesslike classroom behavior   _____

Tests and evaluation reflect classroom lecture,
   discussion and objectives   _____

Availability for consultation   _____

Encouragement of student participation   _____

Assignments clear and concise   _____

Course Related Factors

Appropriateness of project assignments   _____

Value of field trips   _____

Appropriate topic selection for outside assignments   _____

Utilization of supplemental teaching aids, support
   and other activities   _____

Teacher Personal Evaluation

Consideration for differing opinions   _____

Consideration for individuals as persons   _____

Sense of humor   _____

Rating of instructor as compared to other
   college professors   _____

Personal appearance   _____

Instructor's greatest strengths _____

Instructor's greatest weaknesses _____

Suggestions to improve course: _____

SUMMARY

Too often individuals, who have spent a considerable amount of time in the classroom with students, view the role of the faculty member as one fairly lacking pressure and effort. Faculty members who continue to teach the same course will sometimes become lackidaisical in terms of the rigidity of the structure in the classroom situation. This chapter has outlined in some detail the rigorous demands involved in classroom teaching and the significant efforts and energies required prior to taking the first step into the classroom. As was indicated, a teacher who does not plan properly will not be successful. If in fact a teacher plans adequately, then evaluation of those plans is necessary to provide an indication of the validity and the role of the faculty member.

3

Teaching Techniques and Instructional Aids

Chapter 3 is a discussion of some of the most commonly used support systems for classroom teaching. Although the utilization of support systems varies considerably, depending on the differing personality of faculty members, the support described here is typical of most classroom situations. In addition to support systems, this chapter discusses common teaching techniques with suggestions for improvement and techniques for improving communication in the classroom.

TEACHING TECHNIQUES

The Lecture

Although the lecture has long been recognized as one of the more appropriate ways to convey information, there is often a fine line between instructors standing in front of the class "telling" and lecturing. The lecture historically was designed for highly motivated and well-informed people, who were present to hear a specific topic discussed. It has been adapted in recent years to nearly all classroom situations and for that reason is not always as effective as it could be. The lecture can be used effectively in the following ways:

1. *For the development of general interest at the introduction to the main topic of the course.*

2. *In providing additional information to a topic that is being explored in detail in other teaching methods.*

3. *In presenting information on a topic that is not readily available.*

Note that these are very specific applications of the lecture. Although in the first example a description of the faculty member's experiences as an introduction would be apropos, it would not be considered part of the formal lecture. In example 2, a prepared lecture would nearly always accompany a demonstration, project, panel discussion or even a guest lecture presentation. And finally, of course, the lecture is necessary to convey information concerning other written works or developments not available in the course materials.

Advantages. There are several advantages to lecturing:

1. It is an efficient and effective way to communicate content information.

2. It requires little extra physical preparation.

3. It is relatively inexpensive.

4. It is effective with either large or small classes.

5. It is effective in conveying cognitive materials.

Lecturing allows faculty members to maintain eye contact and retain the attention of students. It is probably the most widely used instructional technique in college today. An effective lecturer can convey large amounts of material in a positive atmosphere in a relatively brief period of time.

Disadvantages. There also are disadvantages to the lecture method:

1. It eliminates one of the major elements of a dynamic teacher, that is, variation of activities.
2. It requires that the student vocabulary be equal to that of the instructor.
3. It requires a professional, dynamic presentation by the lecturer in order to hold the student's interest.
4. Few people are really effective lecturers by nature.
5. There is a tendency to end up talking to the class, rather than conducting a well-constructed effective lecture.

Lecture Techniques. There are several methods by which faculty can improve their lecturing capabilities. First, adequate preparation with appropriate support of references, anecdotes, etc., will enhance lecturing effectiveness. Attempting to depend upon memory for such support may prove ineffective, therefore, references, etc., should be formally prepared. Second the lecturer should present a satisfactory physical appearance. Unkempt appearance will negate hours of diligent preparation. Being confident, cool and relaxed with appropriate movement is an art that can be learned with practice. An effective lecturer will cue the class to the major points to be stressed in the presentation and then provide supporting evidence. An effective summary with repetition and reinforcement of important points also is necessary. Whenever possible, the lecture should relate to other topics of interest. It may be a career change they are contemplating or it may simply be the relationship of the course in which they are enrolled to topics in general. As indicated earlier, it is important that vocabulary be classified and definition concerning content be explained. It is not unusual for an effective lecturer to utilize the blackboard or other visual techniques. It is also important that during the lecture appropriate time be allowed for student feedback, questions and discussions.

Question/Answer

Questioning cannot be overused as a tool to evoke classroom participation. Many experienced instructors make it an unwritten rule to call upon every student in the class sometime during each class session. The psychological value in involving students and treating them as if they were worthy of being asked questions, cannot be overlooked. Questions also serve as a motivational factor to many students. General questions directed at the entire class usually are not successful, however. They usually elicit grunts or head nods that really are not meaningful. General questions to the class and then readdressed to an individual are quite effective since they allow students time to phrase an answer.

Advantages. There are several reasons why questions are a good technique for classroom discussion. They include:

1. Stimulation of thought.

2. Arousing curiosity.

3. Stimulating interest.

4. Development of student confidence in expressing themselves.

5. Determination of student progress in the class.

6. Reinforcement of previous points.

7. Evaluation of the preparation of the student.

As indicated at the introduction of this section, there is hardly a disadvantage associated with questioning students in the classroom, if good judgment is exercised in the level of the questions and vocabulary used. Appropriate timing is important. For example, one does not continue to question students who are obviously embarrassed and are having difficulty responding. Some students need to be "brought along" in the classroom. These techniques and concerns of teaching, however, apply to all types of communication and activities in the classroom, not only to question/answer.

One supportive activity that needs to be remembered in questioning is the same that applies to eliciting sales or carrying on communication and other activities of life. That is, one should lead with open-ended questions. Open-ended questions allow students to give a correct or incorrect response or a chance to respond in their own way and vocabulary and possibly to counter with additional questions and concerns. Developing open-ended questions is not a difficult task. Simply asking such open-ended questions as: What do you think of that, Mary? or How does that strike you, John? can very often increase communication in the classroom and lead to more specific types of content questions.

Blackboard Usage

Proper use of the blackboard can be an effective addition to a successful classroom presentation. Too often faculty assume that blackboard technique is relatively simple and/or follow simply the techniques that they observed from their teachers. Chances are the blackboard techniques of previous instructors were bad examples. There are probably *two* categories of blackboard users in the average classroom today:

1. Those who get lost in their work at the blackboard and lose touch with the class, and

2. those who are hesitant or fearful to do extensive blackboard work for fear of losing eye contact with the class.

The blackboard can be an effective motivating device, as well as a learning aid, if used properly.

Principles of Usage. Some of the basic principles of using the blackboard are:

1. It should be used immediately when the class starts. Just the simple writing of the faculty member's name with appropriate spelling is an effective utilization of the

blackboard and does not take much time or lose contact with the class.

2. The blackboard, unlike a piece of paper, should be worked in segments from the right side of the room to the left side for a righthander and the opposite for a lefthander. This allows the information the instructor is writing to be visible to the entire class and not be covered by the body of the instructor.

3. The blackboard is especially useful for listings, allowing the faculty member to write a brief comment on the board, turn and face the class and not lose contact or momentum of the lecture. There was a time a few years ago when all such listings were prepared on handouts. This procedure completely negates the very positive opportunity of involving students with audio and visual communication with the instructor.

4. Items that are to be remembered such as definitions should be placed on the blackboard. This allows the students time to write them down, think about them and again allows the instructor time to pause and look over the class, encouraging comments, etc.

5. Steps in performing operations or listing principles and objectives should be placed on the blackboard.

6. All student assignments, mini quizzes, and diagrams should be placed on the blackboard.

Faculty should make certain that all information on the blackboard is legible and should even occasionally pause and walk to the back of the room to view the board as the students see it. Talking while one is writing on the blackboard, although difficult, is not necessarily a bad technique. One must remember to raise their voice, turn occasionally, and not to write for extended periods of time. When material is placed on the board in proper order, it can then be incorporated as part of the formal lecture.

Another blackboard technique that is very often overlooked in college level work is sending students to the blackboard. Although this may seem elementary and out of place to many college instructors, it is a legitimately good activity. Classes that lend themselves to blackboard participation, such as mathematics and panel presentations, should encourage the use of the blackboard.

The Demonstration

For classes that lend themselves to this technique, the demonstration is a most effective way to teach skills. It is especially effective because it involves communicating with two of the senses: sight and hearing. Psychological researchers claim that nearly 90% of the learning takes place with the involvement of these two senses: Demonstration has other advantages:

1. It is usually motivational.

2. It is an effective technique for varying activities in the classroom.

3. It is an attention getter and can be given to groups or individuals.

4. Demonstrations with today's media can be effectively conducted with large group instruction.

With the recent miniaturization of equipment and the ability to present multi-dimensional visuals, the potential of the demonstration is nearly unlimited. It is probably the most under-used effective teaching tool that exists in today's arena of education.

Good Usage. To be successful, demonstration requires effective preparation on the part of the instructor. Demonstration contains the risk that it will not come off well, but this is a small risk in light of the benefits gained, if it is effective. Students invariably will not be critical of faculty who attempt to utilize complicated techniques if they do not work. They are much more critical of the boring repetitious class. Faculty who adequately prepare for a demonstration should have simulated the presentation prior to the class. This allows one to examine the difficult problems, be alert to the difficulty and even forewarn the students that some steps are particularly difficult. By this simple activity the students will support the instructor and assist in successful demonstration.

One of the most commonly overlooked, simplest errors in conducting a demonstration is inadequate materials, tools, etc. A check list of all demonstration materials should be compiled prior to commencing the demonstration.

Above all, students should be aware of the objectives of the demonstration, which should be reinforced at its conclusion.

The Panel

The panel is an effective activity to stimulate student involvement. The panel, however, must be structured in such a way that there are specific objectives and assignments defined prior to the presentation of the panel. Such activities as stating the issues to be presented and/or defended by each member of the panel, having the students form groups after the presentation of the panel to develop a position is an effective activity. Helping students to develop open-ended questions to pose for the rest of the class to draw conclusions is a very powerful component of panel utilization. Too often panels become a format for under-prepared students simply presenting their own personal opinions. A panel structured in this way is best left undone.

The Project

The project is an effective instrument to provide students the opportunity and the experience of learning outside of the classroom. A properly developed project will give the class a variety of related activities to choose from within their own sphere of interest. Expectations may then be clarified for the students to complete the project activity. Finally, the project should weigh significantly in the final evaluation of the students.

Guest Lecturer

The guest lecturer is an under-utilized technique in most learning institutions. Most communities are rich with individuals who are willing, at a nominal fee or for no fee, to attend classes to share with the students their experience and expertise. The rapidly changing world in which we live makes it nearly impossible for faculty members to remain current on all issues. Inviting individuals who are on the cutting edge of activity in the real world is a very stimulating and informative addition to a class. Again, it is necessary in structuring such a visitation that students are aware of the objectives of the activity.

INSTRUCTIONAL AIDS

Modern technological advances have made it so simple for faculty to incorporate instructional aids in the classroom that there rarely exists a class that cannot benefit from such support. Gone are the days when one wheeled a large film projector into the room, made special arrangements for a screen and called a projectionist to thread the film in order to show a simple 5-8 minute film. Although planning still requires scheduling, ordering and the usual activities, it is far less complex than in the past. In addition to simplicity of operation and convenience, there are available for faculty many support aids that can perform activities not possible with past support systems. In this section a brief description of some of the most commonly used teaching aids is presented.

Overhead Transparencies

The overhead projector in the last several years has become one of the most popular support tools in education. It is unique in that it allows instructors to face the class while showing projections on the screen in normal room lighting. Overhead projectors are inexpensive and often are available in every classroom of modern colleges and universities. Overhead transparencies of notebook size can be easily prepared and retained and are practically indestructible. Some overhead projectors are equipped with a roll that provides instructors with a continuous writing surface. This provides the facility to hold and retain information on the roll in event students later wish to discuss specific points. This is especially useful in mathematics, engineering, etc. Overhead projector transparencies can be prepared by hand at practically no cost and made on many modern copiers. They may also be prepared professionally to provide multi-color or other desired features. It is difficult to conceive of a class in today's modern college or university that cannot in some way utilize overhead transparencies.

Advantages. Overhead transparencies have several advantages over other types of media aids.

1. The equipment is inexpensive and if it is not found in every classroom, usually every department has one or more of these devices available for use.

2. The equipment is easy to use, requiring simply that it be plugged into a wall socket and focused. Sometimes the most difficult operation on an overhead transparency is finding the on/off switch. In modern overheads, it is usually a bar across the front or it has been known to be hidden along the side to the rear of the base.

3. Overhead transparencies are stimulating for the class because they utilize both audio and visual approaches. The visual, of course, is the previous preparation completed by the faculty member.

4. There is no limit to the artistic excellence that can be produced on a transparency. However, most faculty members easily prepare their own transparencies simply by developing materials to be used, either typewritten, handwritten or drawn on a plain piece of 8½ x 11 white paper, taking it to one of the modern copiers on campus and copying off instantaneously an overhead suitable for classroom use. Many times it is worth the extra effort to make a professional looking overhead transparency

simply because they are easily maintained, nearly indestructible and thus can be a permanent part of future presentations.

5. The use of overhead transparencies adds a professional touch to many teaching situations.

6. They can be used in normal classroom conditions, no special lighting is needed and if a screen is not available they can be shown on a wall. No special effects are needed, no special ordering, arranging, etc.

Faculty members who have not utilized overhead transparencies in their classroom presentations should truly write themselves an objective to develop a few for their next teaching assignment. It is one of the few instructional aids that seems to have several advantages and no known disadvantages.

Opaque Projector

When first developed, the opaque projector seemed to be a great addition to classroom instruction. Today, however, the opaque projector is not frequently found in institutions of higher education. For the colleges that do have them, however, they can be a useful device. The opaque projector has unique features in instructional support. It allows one to project on a screen: charts, graphs, maps, etc., directly from a printed document without the additional preparation of slides or overhead transparencies. The size of the image is determined only by the distance from the screen and thus it can be utilized for large group classes. For an enthusiastic teacher willing to spend time in collecting materials used for an opaque projector, it is an effective tool. The greatest disadvantage to the opaque projector seems to be that it is a rather cumbersome instrument and usually special arrangements must be made to obtain one.

Photo Slides

The modern technology of photography has allowed instructors to utilize slide projection as an effective addition to classroom presentation. Thirty-five millimeter slides are a common instructional aid available to nearly all colleges and universities. They have several advantages:

1. They can be produced inexpensively.

2. They are easily stored and used.

3. Many things can be shown on the color slide that cannot be brought to the classroom or shown to students in other ways.

4. They provide a welcome change in pace to any classroom, have a distinct advantage over motion pictures in that they can be stopped for any period of time for discussion, are attractive and usually add an aura of professionalism to the class.

The extra time it takes to prepare and maintain a slide carousel is worth it, especially to faculty who may repeat teaching a course. Many colleges and universities have established slide catalogues for courses that are being taught and instructors should check departmental resources for this support.

Films

Due to the common knowledge of this media only a brief comment will be made at this time. Obviously, movie film has the advantages of being able to take students to places they could not possibly go and put them in positions they could not experience in the classroom. Movie film production is usually professionally done, of high quality and adds a significant degree of professionalism in the class. Some of the disadvantages of movie films are obvious, that is, films can be dated very quickly, they are restrictive in their content in that they must show what is canned and not necessarily what is desired in the class. There is a considerable amount of lead time necessary for scheduling into class and there are special arrangements to be made for their showing.

The advantages of utilizing movie films outweighs the disadvantages, however. Most colleges and universities have their own film library or at least a catalogue from which films can be ordered through a processing service or directly from an agency. Faculty members should plan utilization of the films prior to the class so that an adequate time for obtaining them is available.

Video Tape

Probably the most exciting instructional aid to come along since the introduction of movie film is video tapes. For institutions that have video tape playback units, the video tape is probably the best of all the instructional aids available. There are several advantages. They are:

1. Easy to operate. Simply the insertion of a cartridge into an easily operable unit.

2. They can be purchased for nearly any content; films may be converted to video tape and new subjects and topics developed.

3. Video tapes are relatively simple to modify in terms of updating content.

4. They can be any length with no inconvenience, they can be stopped or started to utilize them as an integral part of class discussion.

5. They are inexpensive.

Video tapes provide all the advantages of movie film, but none of the disadvantages. With the development of modern consumer technology it is possible for faculty to make their own video tapes of very high quality.

Computer Assisted Instruction (CAI) —
Computer Managed Instruction (CMI)

A very brief comment will be made here concerning the computer and its role in assisting faculty in classroom teaching. What was thought a few years back to be an addition to the educational world that would revolutionize the teaching learning process has had very little effect on the everyday classroom. This is not to say that it will not have greater effect in the future; however, as a medium to assist the average adjunct faculty member, computer assistance does not exist. There are many reasons that the computer instruction movement did not develop. Some of them are quite simple. The original content of many of the programs which had to be prepared by a professional programmer was not relevant or accurate in terms of the needs of the classroom. Too much time was spent trying to make content in important subjects look like games in the eyes of the students. In addition, the development of such programs is rather expensive to update, trial run, correct and quality control. Not only are considerable funds expended, but the time lag to usability is significant. This is not to say that much information is not available in these two areas. Faculty members who are sincerely interested in being on the cutting edge of state-of-the-art technology may wish to pursue these supports. There will be no attempt in this publication to do so.

One must keep in mind that there are two distinct areas in which the computer relates to instruction. Computer assisted instruction, usually called CAI, is simply the utilization of computer programs and techniques that can be applied to content or preparation that is already presented by other means. Sometimes this method is valuable in problem solving or situations where large quantities of data such as demographic studies are handled.

The other area involving the computer in instruction is called computer managed instruction (CMI). This area of instructional technology allows students to interact with the computer, communicating back and forth, perceiving cues and responses from the computer in a complete learning situation. As was indicated earlier, neither of these systems has made a major impact on the teaching profession.

4

Teaching Adult Students

Although it is difficult for faculty members to adequately plan in a standard way for all classes (because each class has a unique personality), there are fundamental activities that can be utilized to motivate students. One must keep in mind, however, that motivation is not a static state and requires constant reassessment throughout one's teaching career. Techniques which may have worked for past classes or past years may not be the appropriate technique for the present class.

Motivation

The writer recalls, after many years of teaching college students, of being faced with a class that simply would not come to life. Admittedly it was a Friday night class, however, one might expect that in such a class, highly motivated students might be enrolled. They were, however, very tired students and many of them were enrolled simply to pick up additional credits. After teaching the class about three weeks and experiencing very little student response, on the spur of the moment on the third evening, I simply stated, "We must start communicating. I would like each of you at this time to turn to a person near you, introduce yourself and tell this person that you are going to help them get through this course, no matter how difficult it is. That you will be there to help them in the future, whenever they get stuck and that the two of you (by helping each other) can make it through the course." This seemingly simple technique, in this particular class, worked wonders. The students became acquainted with someone they didn't know previously, and surprisingly in many cases, found someone who really *could* help them get through the course. For the remainder of the course, when things were slow or heavy, I needed simply to say "let's take a few minutes and get together with our partner and work this thing through." They immediately would team up and before long teams of two were getting together in groups of four to assist each other. When blackboard work was given, two people would go to the board instead of one. This is an example of trying basic techniques of motivation. In this case it worked. It may not work every time, but it was not a technique that I had in my repertoire prior to that time.

So in introducing this topic, *motivation of adult students,* I am simply saying that you may have to try some things that are not in the book.

One definition of motivation is:

> *an activity by one person designed to stimulate or arouse a state within a second person or a group that under appropriate circumstances initiates or regulates activities.*

There is nothing in this definition that says it applies only to college age students. We must assume that the classes we are teaching are an appropriate circumstance and that adults are included. For purposes in the classroom, an adult is anyone who shows up for class.

False Assumptions. First, there are some false assumptions concerning adults that must be put to rest. *There is the assumption* *that older adults have passed their peak learning period.* This assumption simply is not a major concern of faculty. Almost any adult can learn if given the appropriate amount of time. Studies have shown that there is no significant brain cell erosion until late in old age. One researcher found in a study in 1970 that the typical adult conducts five learning projects each year — each of which takes more than 100 hours.

The second false assumption is that adults who did poorly in school will tend to do poorly later. This is unequivocally false. Informal learning tends to bridge the gap. Adults who did poorly in high school will tend to lack confidence and this should be a concern of the instructor, but is certainly not an indicator of later learning capability. In the study cited above concerning learning projects, it was determined that 79-98% of the adults who participate in the learning activities only 12-31% were officially enrolled in a formal course of study. Thus, older adults have continued to learn throughout the years without attending college classes. Adjunct faculty members should feel confident in assuring older students, who have been out of the classroom for several years, that they can and will do well.

Special Considerations. There are some special considerations for adults of which we must be aware:

1. First, *adults will vary in how quickly and efficiently information is processed and learned.* Everyone has heard the traditional statement it takes him or her longer to grasp it, but once they get it, they learn it well. Actually, he or she doesn't learn it any better if it takes longer, it just happens to be part of the learning process for this person. The amount of time to process new information varies considerably with individuals, however, the effect it has on retention of information is affected more by the reinforcement provided the students in the instructional process.

2. A second special consideration; one that should be of

great importance to adjunct faculty members, is the fact that *adult students vary significantly in terms of their experience and psychological set.* Adult student experiences can be of great assistance to faculty if utilized properly in the classroom. For example, if one is teaching about financial investment and a banker is in the class, the individual could be a valuable resource to the class and other students. There is a danger, however, that the activity may impede the learning process as well as help it. Very often experienced individuals in the class will have a story to tell of their past, but it may not be relevant to the goals and objectives of the class.

3. *There is research that states that most adults have stable, short-term memories throughout life, but experience some loss in the ability to store the information, especially when it requires recall of stored information.* Thus, older students will tend to make more errors due to forgetting rather than mistakes. This is an important criteria in assignment of grades. It is also important to keep in mind for courses involving concepts and abstract ideas or prerequisites. Older students may often seem confused when in fact they are suffering from a recall problem.

4. A factor to be considered in teaching adults is that *long-term memory is often retained better with age.* The implications here are significant. One should not make the assumption that older persons, who appear brilliant in discussing the modification of the internal combustion engine of the 1940s, are in fact so brilliant. It may simply be long-term recall and the student may be embarrassed if called upon to discuss in such detail contemporary topics.

5. The final consideration is one which is familiar to all experienced faculty members. *It is the commonly held belief that adult students come to class motivated.*

Although it is true that most adult students are achievement oriented and are highly motivated to return to college, they are not necessarily motivated for a particular class. In fact, the reverse may be true. Adult students are faced with many distractions that do not affect the lives of college age students. Adult students may be distracted by such important considerations as: buying a home, worrying about children, going through a divorce, etc. Also, it must be realized that many adult students are in class simply for social purposes. Sometimes this attendance is therapeutic in nature, sometimes it is simply to expand social horizons and meet other people. Adults frequently enroll in class because they are told to do so or have their tuition paid by their employer. Many times this places an additional burden on students who are having difficulty achieving grades good enough for reimbursement. Finally, the perpetual search for job change skills, and upgrading of competencies is a concern of many adult students.

These factors contribute to the difficulty of teaching adult students.

Maslow's Hierarchy

Faculty will find it impossible to consider all of the factors that affect the motivation of their students. It is appropriate, therefore, that we find refuge in a time honored theory of learning development called "Maslow's Hierarchy of needs." Maslow's hierarchy of needs states that the basic needs of human beings fall into five categories: psychological, safety, love and belonging, esteem and self-actualization. It is upon these factors that the motivation principles of this section be considered.

Maslow's hierarchy is defined as follows:

1. PHYSIOLOGICAL needs — *feeling good physically with appropriate food and shelter.*

2. SAFETY — *the feeling of security in one's environment.*

3. LOVE AND BELONGING OR THE SOCIAL NEED — *fulfilling the basic family and social role.*

4. ESTEEM — *the status and respect of a positive self-image.*

5. SELF-ACTUALIZATION — *growth of the individual.*

These needs are developed in a hierarchial mode. That is, growth and esteem will not become evident if the previous three needs have not been met.

The fact that Maslow's needs are hierarchial is a major problem for adjunct faculty. Attempting to address the needs of esteem and self-actualization in the classroom, when psychological, safety and love, and belonging needs have not been met, is a monumental task. In fact, the lack of fulfillment of the basic needs may interfere with the learning process itself. This interference may manifest itself in anti-social behavior that all faculty are faced with at one time or another. Some characteristics of this behavior include:

- Apparent lack of interest on the part of the student.
- General lack of class response.
- A lack of communication with the instructor and other students.
- Aggressive behavior.
- Attempted verbal domination of the class or the opposite — withdrawal from class.
- Constant complaints about the instructor and the college.
- Absence.
- Tardiness.
- Complaints about the class in general.

The challenge becomes: how does one in a short period of time, teaching on a part-time basis to part-time students, overcome all these barriers. The fact is that one does not overcome all of these barriers. In fact, if instructors attempt to take the time to pick apart each of the unmet needs of each of the students they would have very little time to work toward the goals and objectives of the course. There is, however, an important factor in support of the instructor, as he or she moves on with the teaching learning process. It is the fact that the need to achieve appears to be a basic need in human beings. The need to achieve, an intrinsic motivator that usually overcomes all of or most of the other distractions of learning, is the factor upon which successful teachers capitalize. Although student achievement has not received the publicity or attention of educational psychologists that other motivators have, it is still the basic motivator of students of all ages. There is little faculty can do to help students to meet their psychological, safety and love, and belonging needs; the need for *esteem* and *self-actualization*, however, which are essentially achievement, are areas in which teaching strategies can be developed. It is these two areas that a major portion of the motivational techniques and processes are addressed in this chapter.

Esteem. Esteem is the status and respect with which human beings are regarded. Thus, activities faculty members incorporate that assist students in building status and self-respect, will support fulfillment of the esteem need. This is accomplished by providing an environment in which students can experience success in their learning endeavors. *Many learning theorists claim that success in itself is the solution to motivation and learning.* For some classes this is a significant change from the norm. Some classes appear to be designed to eliminate certain students.

One of the great fallacies in teaching is often stated by students who have succeeded in classes where other students have dropped out. That is, the offstated observation "that prof was tough, but he/she was really good." This may or may not be true. The point is that being tough has absolutely no relationship to being good. Too often the reverse of this statement is generalized upon and some faculty concentrate on toughness as a substitution for good teaching. There is no evidence to indicate that "tough teachers" are better than teachers not considered so tough. It is especially discouraging to marginal students who are working hard when the chances for success experiences are negated by the instructor's desire to be tough.

Success experiences are accomplished in many ways. Compiled here are some suggestions that can be incorporated in classroom instruction to assist students to experience success:

- *Make certain that students are aware of your expectations.* That is, students should be provided with course objectives in written form that tell them what they are expected to accomplish.

- *Inform students precisely what is expected of them.* This means not only the work or the knowledge necessary for them to complete the course content, but also the time commitment required.

- *Give students non-verbal encouragement whenever possible.* There are many ways this can be accomplished. Eye contact with students can very often elicite positive response. Gestures are important. Gestures pointing upward are positive, downward are negative. The smile, a nod of the head, just looking at students with the feeling that they are working in a pleasant environment is in itself effective non-verbal encouragement.

- *Provide students with positive reinforcement at every opportunity possible.* Simple techniques such as quizzes when grades are not taken, quizzes with the intent that most or all students will succeed, as well as quizzes as a supplementary part of grading and evaluation are effective positive reinforcers. Comments and notes written on hand-in papers, tests, and projects are very effective positive feedback components. Of course, the ideal form of positive reinforcement is provided through individual conferences and informal conferences with students at chance meetings or on a scheduled basis.

- *Provide a structured situation in which the students will feel comfortable.* The laissez-faire classroom is generally a lazy classroom. The experiences of the early 1960s and 1970s resulted in many dissatisfied students who really did not achieve to their capacity. It is generally agreed that the structured setting with students participating in activities, and in some degree the aims and objectives, is much better than the "what shall we do today" approach.

- *Allow outside experiences and resources provided by the students to be discussed.* Some of the greatest talents in the classroom are the students. Students in class, who may not be particularly adept at the subject, may have significant contributions and accomplishments to share in other areas. One of the greatest builders of esteem is to allow students to share their success experiences with others.

It should be noted in this section on building esteem that very little is mentioned concerning content. *That is because it is generally agreed that most failures in college courses are due to barriers that are not related to content.*

Self-Actualization. Self-actualization is the need for individuals to grow. Obviously growth cannot be achieved if there has not been past achievement and in most cases past success. Self-actualization is the fifth and the highest of Maslow's hierarchy. Self-actualization is much more difficult to accomplish than the previous four factors. However, the suggestions below indicate some of the behaviors that can be affected in the classroom to assist in the student growth process.

1. *Each class should offer a challenge to each student.* Challenges are presented in a variety of modes. If they are insurmountable challenges they are barriers. Therefore, it is important that faculty plan activities as challenges rather than frustration experiences. Grades are

challenges, however, grades must be achieveable or they
cause frustration. Course credit and obtaining the same is
a challenge. Most students even though they may not
achieve the grade desired, will feel satisfied if they obtain
the credit for which they are working and they must
understand that the credit itself is more valuable than the
grade obtained. Assigning incompletes, additional time
for projects, etc., are techniques utilized to assist students
in obtaining credit for the work they have contributed.
Questions in class, if properly phrased, can be
appropriately challenging. Above all, teachers must be
careful that questions do not lead to embarrassment of the
students. The ultimate challenge in the classroom is, of
course, problem solving. Problem solving techniques vary
greatly depending upon the subject matter. Although it is
impossible in this brief essay to discuss in detail the
ramifications of problem solving, this challenge does not
lend itself solely to scientific and mathematics classes. It
can also be utilized in many of the liberal arts-discussion
courses through the use of professional journals,
literature, and outside projects.

2. *Students want to be treated as individuals.*
   If there was a lesson learned from the unrest of the 1960s it
   was the realization that many colleges during the post
   World War II crunch of students through the 1950s had
   unintentionally slipped into an operational mode where
   students were treated as masses and groups rather than
   as individuals. The relevant education theme was not as
   important as the depersonalized education theme.
   Students can be treated as individuals in many ways.
   Individual conferences and the development of a system
   to allow students to get to know their instructors and other
   students is important. Many experienced faculty
   members do not hesitate to share with students their

home phone number. Usually they are quite amazed at how seldom students actually use it.

3. *Be cautious not to prejudge students.*
Unfortunately, stereotyping still exists in classrooms today. Faculty must make every effort not to "type" classes as good or bad classes or students as good or bad students. Such stereotyping will affect grading and attitudes toward the students. Also, there is a very good chance that the judgment may be incorrect. There is no place for stereotypes in education.

4. *Students wish to be treated as adults.*
Many of today's students hold powerful positions in business and industry in the community. It is difficult for them to look upon the teacher as someone superior. To these people the instructor is just someone in a different role.

5. *Give consideration to students' personal problems when appropriate.*
Giving adult students personal consideration simply means that attendance, paper deadlines, etc., may be flexible when one is faced with realities of life of adult students. However, faculty should constantly guard against becoming counselors to the many personal problems of students. It is not possible for an instructor to deal with all of the problems of the students and still be effective in the major role of teaching the class.

6. *Provide every opportunity for flexibility in the classroom.*
Rigid rules concerning attendance, tardiness, test makeups, etc., usually are demeaning to students, usually are not successful, and often are legally invalid. The flexible instructor is the more effective teacher. Flexibility has absolutely nothing to do with authority. Faculty always have authority in the classroom and can exert it at

any time they wish. It is not necessary to exert authority in picky areas such as tardiness.

The previous paragraphs have outlined general observations concerning the building of success experiences and the self-actualization of students. If instructors spend just 20% of their time on techniques related to the behaviors described here, the rewards will be exciting.

In summary, it can be observed that motivation is basically intrinsic. It is inside the beholder. It may be stimulated by external forces and must be cultivated by the student. Instructors cannot develop a set of procedures to guarantee motivation of students. Faculty can, however, be an important intervening variable in the motivational process. Faculty action and behavior will be influential to the motivational process of each student in the classroom. *The best way to motivate students is to be a motivated teacher.*

Teaching Strategies

Although motivating students is probably the most important task that faculty encounter, being prepared with tried and proven strategies to address student needs is an equally important function for instructors. Although strategies vary considerably among different faculty members, there are some basic principles involved in teaching that are applicable to most situations. This section will discuss some of these principles.

1. *The instructor is a facilitator of learning.*
   Unlike the traditions of the past and the philosophy under which many present day teachers obtained their education, the teacher of today is not required to be a possessor of all the knowledge available for a discipline or course or be able to answer all the questions. Successful teachers today find that the most effective role is acting as a facilitator of learning. Knowing how to develop learning skills is more important to today's students than knowing

all the answers. Obviously, the reason for this is that over a period of time many of the answers change but once students have mastered the techniques of learning there is no limit to their capacity. Although this may appear to be a simple approach to teaching, it carries with it an additional responsibility — that faculty must become involved in learning as a profession, must read literature on learning, make a study of the varied student types, learning styles, and factors that affect student learning.

2. *Teaching effectiveness is situational.*
Experienced teachers find that no two classes are alike. One may use all the historically proven teaching techniques and even some that are not historically proven to bring out students in classes, yet the effectiveness will vary depending upon the situation and the students. Obviously, students who are highly motivated to complete a program or achieve a recognizably high quality grade point average will present a different situation than students who are struggling to learn. Yet sometimes students striving for high achievement are in many ways more difficult to teach than students who are seeking to find themselves. Each class will develop its own personality. It is to the teacher's advantage to make it a happy personality.

3. *Understand the teaching situation.*
Many individuals reading this handbook will have experienced the meaning of this statement. Instructors who have been assigned a variety of adjunct faculty assignments in different types of institutions will attest to the fact that there is significant difference in assignments. If one is teaching in an open-door community college, one must be cognizant of the fact that students with a variety of backgrounds will be attending classes. Individuals teaching advanced classes in open-

door colleges or classes requiring prerequisites or in selective programs will find the characteristics of students very similar to that of institutions that have higher admission standards. It is important that faculty assess these factors in preparing for their teaching assignment. Some questions that might be asked in making such a preparation are: Is this class part of a competitive program? Are the goals clarified for both the institution and the student? Can student projects be developed so that the interest of students can be adequately explored? And is the size of the class a factor? Remember a very large class is limited in the number of techniques that can be utilized in the teaching process, whereas in a small class there is a tendency to digress and fall into conversation rather than instruction.

4. *You are an actor or actress and you are on stage.*
   Remember to use humor delicately. Do not attempt jokes of any kind. Don't let compassion become sympathy and you need not be concerned about exerting your authority. It is there when you need it.

5. *Allow for student individual differences.*
   The diversity of university and college students in any type of institution today is significant. Years ago just the identification of someone as a "college student" would to a large degree describe the type of person. Obtaining information about students without offending them is important to faculty if consideration for individual differences is to be accomplished. The information card at the beginning of the course is effective, however, students should not be asked for more information than they are given concerning the instructor.

6. *Vary teaching activities.*
   In the author's opinion, varying activities in the teaching process is the most important technique that can be used.

Not only does changing activities motivate students, it has the best chance of addressing the needs of the diverse student population. In addition, it is stimulating to faculty preparation and assists them to remain "sharp" in their teaching activities. In fact, one might even vary activities to the point of trying unique and creative techniques and strategies just to see if they will work.

7. *Develop a supportive climate.*
Students must be made to feel that instructors are there to support them in the learning process and are not a part of the elimination process. To students who come to college with a background of failure, this is very important. There are several things that faculty can do to develop a supportive climate. They include: know the students by name; respond to them as individuals, not as a group or a class; be understanding and compassionate rather than authoritative; give evidence of leading and learning while using expressions such as "what do you think of that?" and finally, involve the students in planning and goal setting to clarify expectations. Make certain that the students understand exactly upon what their grade will be assigned. Don't force the students to psych out the teachers for a grade.

8. *Be sensitive to barriers.*
Students bring to class many barriers to their learning. Although as is indicated elsewhere in this publication, faculty cannot become overly sympathetic in their feelings with individual students, there are many general barriers that must be recognized to be an effective teacher. These include:
a. Unsuccessful previous educational experiences on the part of the student. Development of activities leading to early success will help to minimize the effects of previous failures. Being alert to early signs of failure

and assisting students in techniques of notetaking, test taking, library procedures, etc., will provide supportive confidence needed by such students.

b. The time barrier. Discuss time commitments with students at the beginning of the course. The barrier of time is an important one to working adult students and/or housewives returning who have other responsibilities. Be fair and realistic. Don't use scare tactics in terms of the number of hours they will be required to put in.

c. College procedures. Becoming knowledgeable of policies so that they can be passed on to students will help ally this barrier. How are books checked out in the library; what about dropping and adding classes; where do they get a student ID; activity card; what are the procedures to taking part in student activities; buying books; where is the financial aid office, the counseling office; knowing answers to these questions will help eliminate the frustrations of higher education for the students.

d. Lack of understanding their limitations and strengths. If weaknesses in reading, writing, or math skills are detected they should be brought in the open with the student in private conference. Knowing where students can obtain help or referral is important. Almost all colleges today have some type of remedial or refresher courses. The classroom instructor is the person who will first come across such deficiencies and will be in an important position of assisting students.

e. Stress. As is indicated elsewhere in this publication, students exhibiting irresponsible behavior may be reacting to deficiencies in the first three factors of Maslow's hierarchy: psychological, safety, and love and belonging needs. Being careful to avoid confrontation and being considerate is important in stressful situations.

f. Physically Handicapped individuals. Remember, many handicapped students do not wish to share their handicap as a public issue. At the beginning of class it is a good technique to simply comment if anyone needs special seating, etc., to see you after class and it can be arranged. Students can then take their new seats at the beginning of the second class while there is still confusion without great attention being paid to the issue.

5

Testing and Grading

Testing and grading practices are of major importance to most students. Unfortunately, our educational system has not clearly defined the purposes of tests and testing. Ideally, the testing process should be one in which successes are measured as part of a developmental process that informs both students and teachers of the progress made in the teaching-learning situation. Unfortunately, in practice, testing is used for many other purposes and anxieties are unnecessarily raised. For example, testing is often used to: eliminate students and people from promotions, classes, courses, programs, colleges, careers, etc. Testing also is often used to determine the rank of students in their class or in the program regardless of their major. These and many other related factors have a direct effect upon student behaviors during the testing process.

Faculty must make every effort to prepare students for the testing in the course. This process starts by informing students at the beginning of the class of the testing procedure; when tests will be given and upon what they will be based. Too many times students are heard to criticize instructors with the statement "they didn't test over what they talked about in class."

Let's review the ideal situation under which tests are given. Ideally, tests are intended for the following reasons:

1. To reveal to students their areas of strength.

2. To reveal to the instructor the student's progress.

3. To provide motivation for students.

4. To help instructors evaluate their teaching.

5. To provide a basis upon which grades are determined.

6. As a means of evaluation of students in terms of their professional and career goals.

Too often students and faculty relate the testing process as one for determination of grades only, when in fact there are more lasting and important reasons for testing.

Most experienced teachers are familiar with the major types of tests. The most commonly used tests in colleges are the multiple choice, the essay and recall. There is little attention given at the college level to performance tests, oral tests, written tests or short answer. For that reason the major emphasis in this description of testing will be placed upon the tests that are used most extensively. There are many types of tests: personality, aptitude, ability, career choice, diagnostic, etc., not normally used in the classroom that will not be discussed here. The major tests of concern to faculty members is the achievement tests.

ACHIEVEMENT TESTS

Achievement tests are devised to determine if students have achieved the objectives that the course intended. It is intended that achievement will reflect a measure of the growth that occurred in the student during the class. More specifically, it is hopeful that such growth can be determined in terms of the cognitive, psychomotor and affective domains. Achievement tests are developed in many formats. The most basic achievement test, of course, is the written response. Most of the various tests known to faculty members, that is, multiple choice, essay, etc., call upon achievement as their basis. This section will address primarily these tests. Before continuing with the discussion of tests, however, we will first discuss two important characteristics of good tests. They are validity and comprehensiveness.

Validity. The validity of a test is determined by answering the very simple question, "Are we testing what we should be testing?" Probably in many of the classes that part-time faculty attended as undergraduates, the validity of tests was often in question. Too often course preparations were not structured in a way that testing was consistent with the discussions that took place in class. In modern class planning which requires that each class have objectives, validity becomes less of a problem. *To maintain validity in the testing situation, faculty must simply be certain that their evaluation instrument and questions are based upon the objectives written for the course.*

Comprehensiveness. Obviously, the comprehensiveness of a test is of importance in the evaluation of students. A test that is not comprehensive will neither be objective or valid. To test students on a small sample of what has been taught during the course is unfair to students who may not completely grasp that segment of the course, but has mastery over the class in general. *Again, comprehensiveness is not a problem if objectives are written that cover a broad spectrum of the major purposes of the course and the test is developed for those objectives.* One must be careful to make certain that the test adequately samples the universe of the content which has been taught. The development of a broad body of questions covering the comprehensiveness of the course and then selecting from those questions at evaluation time can assure comprehensiveness without repetition of the same questions.

Essay Tests

Essay tests are one of the most popular of college tests. They are effective at any level of the hierarchy. That is, analysis and synthesis are easily incorporated into the essay questions. Although essay tests require considerable time for students to respond, they do give an in-depth perspective in terms of overall student ability.

There are several factors to remember when writing test questions that require essay answers. First and foremost is the fact that essay questions should be related to the objectives written for the course. They should, if possible, be related to the objectives written at the analysis or synthesis level. Secondly, essay questions should incorporate a significant amount of content. Realizing that the students will take a long time to respond, questions should not be posed so that excessive time is spent on trivial matters. Finally, one must be certain that in terms of vocabulary, content, subject covered, etc., the student has sufficient background to respond adequately to the question being asked and that the question queried is not ambiguous or deceiving in any way.

Essay questions, if constructed and graded properly, are the most accurate of the possible testing procedures. Although in recent years most teachers have resorted to some type of objective grading system, the essay question still leaves considerable latitude for students of ability to express themselves beyond the minimum competencies required. Although this also runs the risk of allowing professional jargon, it usually allows some degree of subjectiveness and can be used in a positive manner if controlled by the objectives of the course. Individuals who develop a high degree of skill in writing essay questions find that they can allow for a degree of flexibility.

Grading of essay questions presents the greatest problem. One must keep in mind that essay questions are asking students to be objective, yet to generalize. The appropriate way to judge an essay response is to write the response from the faculty viewpoint, list important comments in priority. Assignment of points to the prioritized criteria will then lend to grading criteria.

The instructor must be cautious, however, that essay questions do not ask for student opinions. Theoretically, if one is merely asking an opinion, every student should get a perfect score.

Advantages of Essay Questions. The advantages of essay questions are enumerated below:

1. They can provide in-depth coverage of material or content presented in the class.

2. They allow students maximum utilization of their capabilities in responding to an issue.

3. They are quick and simple to prepare.

4. They can be changed from class to class without greatly affecting the purpose of the question.

Disadvantages of Essay Questions. There are several disadvantages to essay questions:

1. They are restrictive in the breadth of the subject matter being measured.

2. They are time consuming for the students.

3. They have a tendency to weigh too heavily a specific part of the course at the expense of other parts.

4. They present the burden of handwriting, spelling, vocabulary, and grammar upon the student.

5. They have a tendency to lean toward subjectivity in evaluation.

6. They are difficult to grade.

Multiple Choice Tests

Multiple choice questions are probably the most widely used testing technique in college today. With the implementation of computer scoring and computer assisted storage of questions, the development and maintenance of such tests are relatively simple. In addition, item analysis techniques, validity, objectivity and comprehensiveness can be maintained with multiple choice tests.

Advantages of Multiple Choice. Multiple choice questions have several advantages that have led to their popularity. They are as follows:

1. They can be used to cover a broad scope of work in a short period of time.

2. They measure the ability of students to recognize appropriate responses rather than to recall facts. (This is a significant benefit to older students who sometimes become confused with the recall of things they have learned.)

3. They are significantly more valid than true/false or other related types of questions that have a 50% chance of being correct.

4. Students can be tested at the analysis and synthesis level.

5. They are easy to grade.

6. They are easily made to be comprehensive in nature.

Disadvantages of Multiple Choice. There are some disadvantages to multiple choice questions that must be of concern to those preparing the tests. They are as follows:

1. There is a tendency to construct most responses at the knowledge level.

2. The questions are time consuming and difficult to develop if validity is maintained.

3. They provide for some guessing and elimination of responses.

4. They rely primarily upon recall and memory.

Preparing Multiple Choice Questions. The development of valid multiple choice questions is a significant challenge to the teacher. The best way to assure valid multiple choice responses is to develop a series of questions as quizzes that are not graded. Listed below are several suggestions for the construction of multiple choice questions.

1. Compose multiple choice responses with four possible answers to minimize the guess factor.

2. Do not include impossible answers, they are easily eliminated.

3. Do not muddy the activity with the use of such responses as none of the above or all of the above.

4. Be consistent with the response format. That is, capitalization, punctuation, etc.

5. Do not use qualifiers such as always, or general qualifiers such as usually.

6. State all the questions in a positive form.

7. Keep all multiple choice statements of approximately the same length.

Recall Tests

Straight recall tests are used infrequently in college level work. Recall items may be posed as simple questions, completion or writing of brief responses. Although recall is involved in nearly any kind of evaluation system, specific recall of words that would ally straight memorization usually is not incorporated in college level evaluation.

Advantages of Recall Tests. In event the instructor wishes to utilize recall questions there are some advantages. They include:

1. They are relatively simple to grade and construct.

2. Recall questions can address numerous areas in a broad field of content.

3. They require a specific recall rather than a guess such as may occur in true/false and multiple choice.

Disadvantages of Recall Tests. Some of the reasons that straight recall is not used include:

1. They may be time consuming to the student, that is, extensive time can be used attempting to recall something for which they have a mental block.

2. Subjectivity is introduced into the grading of similar responses.

3. It is nearly impossible to measure analysis or synthesis activities.

Suggestions for Development of Recall Questions. To utilize recall questions, there is some basic information that must be kept in mind. It includes:

1. Give information concerning the material being sought prior to the blank for the answer.

2. Clearly qualify the information so that students know specifically the required response, that is, eliminate generalizations.

3. Attempt to solicit responses at the analysis and synthesis level.

4. Pose the question in such a way that only one correct response can be given.

5. Allow sufficient and equal space for all responses so that the space does not tip off the response.

True/False Tests

True/false questions are not commonly used at the college level. Although they may have their place in sampling of student responses or a learning activity, they generally are not acceptable as being objective or valid. In event there is opportunity for their use, some suggestions are listed below.

Advantages of True/False. There are some advantages to true/false questions that must be considered for special circumstances. They include:

1. A large number and diversity of questions may be asked about a specific topic.

2. They are good to stimulate students and give lower ability students a chance at success.

3. They are simple and time saving to develop.

4. They are valid if only two possible answers exist.

5. They are non-threatening and familiar to students.

6. They are easily scored.

Disadvantages of True/False. The disadvantage and limitation of true/false questions are numerous:

1. Even with the allowance for correction factors, true/false questions encourage guessing.

2. It is difficult to construct brief, complete true/false statements.

3. Equal grading weight is equal for minor factors, as well as significant points.

4. They are not appropriate for elaboration or discussion.

5. They tend to test the lowest level of knowledge with no consideration for analysis and synthesis.

6. They are typically low in validity and reliability due to the guess factor.

Constructing True/False Items. If one has elected to utilize true/false questions as part of their evaluation system, there are several factors to consider in the development of these questions. They are:

1. Avoid unclear statements with ambiguous words or trick questions.

2. Develop questions that require responses beyond the knowledge or the rote memorization level.

3. Avoid patterning answers with long strings of trues or falses or direct alteration.

4. Avoid direct quotes as they will tip off responses.

5. Avoid specific descriptors or adjectives that might tip off responses.

GRADING

Basic Rules. Grading of students is probably the most difficult task for faculty. All of the elements of teaching: preparation, presentation, student activity, are reflected in the grading process. In addition, in an era of accountability, teachers are sometimes called upon to justify grades with documentation. Thus, the establishment of firm criteria for grading is necessary.

There are some general rules that are helpful in establishing the grading process. They are listed below.

1. **Communicate criteria.**

   Faculty should communicate the grading criteria usually the first or second session. A suggestive chart for this activity is shown in figure 7. Every effort should be made to allow students to respond to the grading format in the process, before the first evaluation is given.

2. **Include criteria other than test scores.**

   Factors other than test scores should be included in the students' grades. This is especially true in social science courses where content criteria and problem solving is not easy to assess. For example, if it is important for students to communicate or express ideas, then class participation *should* be a part of the grading criteria. If a written paper or a project is part of the grade, students should be advised of the weight of the project applied to the grade. If laboratory demonstrations are part of the course, their value should be made known.

3. **Avoid irrevelant factors.**

   Avoid introducing irrelevant factors into the grading process. Including attendance and tardiness in the grading criteria is unwise. Many experienced teachers feel that if students possess the knowledge and show that they have reached the objectives of the course, they should be evaluated appropriately. The insistence that one must sit in a classroom a certain number of minutes and hear things they already know is a bit unreal. This is especially true in teaching adults who may have significant career and business experience but not have received the official credit or course work. Introducing attendance in class as part of the grading criteria simply breeds animosity on the part of the student and is very difficult to justify on the part of the instructor.

4. **Weigh grading criteria carefully.**

   One should be careful not to overweigh certain segments of the grading criteria. For example, if one is to develop a grading plan such as shown in the diagram in figure 7, and then allow 90% of the grade to count for the final examination, they have probably defeated the purpose of comprehensive grading. Equally important is the weighing of extra credit for extra work. If such a technique is used it should not penalize the students who do not feel it necessary to do extra work.

5. **Grade students on their achievement, not other students.**

   Grading should be based upon criteria of the course and not upon other students' scores. Bill Frye (Greive, *et al.,* 1983) best explains this in his discussion of grading. Several years ago, many teachers utilized a technique called grading on the curve. This technique essentially distributed all students in all classes on a normal curve and said that 2.15% will get A's and F's, 13.59% will get B's and D's, and 68.26% will get C's. This system placed students in competition with each other irregardless of the effectiveness of the classroom learning situation. In recent years criterion based grading has found favor. Criterion based grading evaluates the student independent of other students based upon the criteria of the course. The criteria of the course are the objectives written for the course. Thus, quite simply the students should be graded upon the degree to which they have completed the objectives of the course and not how other students achieved. Thus, if all students reach all of the objectives they all should receive passing scores.

Evaluation Plan

In order to clearly define and delineate the criteria for assignment of grades, it is helpful if one first develops an evaluation plan. An evaluation plan is a very simple device usually developed in chart and worksheet form. The plan contains all of the factors that apply to the evaluation of the students. Across from these factors is listed the percentage of weight that will be assigned to the various factors. A third column then indicates the points received for each factor. A sample plan is shown in figure 7.

Figure 7

Evaluation Chart

Grade Factors	Percent of Final Grade	Possible Points	Points Received
Tests	60	90	_____
Paper	20	30	_____
Project	10	15	_____
Class Participation	10	15	_____
Totals	100	150	_____

Please note that any number of factors can be included in the first column. For example, a technical course might include laboratory work, laboratory demonstrations, completion of projects, etc. An evaluation worksheet allows one to weigh the factors that apply to a specific class with the flexibility of changing them when necessary. Obviously, when developing the chart it is necessary that the percent of weight total 100% for the course. In order to complete the evaluation worksheet, one must simply assign the number of points possible to each of the categories. Keep in mind that the total number of points may or may not total 100 depending upon the application involved (the example shows 150). It remains simply then to add a fourth column entitled "points received." Points received, obviously, are the number of points earned by the student in each category.

This system allows faculty flexibility in establishing documented criteria for assignment of grades. Faculty members may, for example, arbitrarily pick the total number of points desired to equal 100%. This then can be converted to the number of points necessary to be earned through each of the factors by multiplying by the percentage. An additional step is for one to simply take that number of points divided by the number of activities in each of the factors to determine the value for each activity, even to the level of determining the value of each test question. This documentation clearly indicates to the students the process by which evaluation is conducted in a businesslike and professional manner.

Item Analysis

A quick and semi-scientific method of checking the validity of exam questions is to utilize a technique called item analysis. Although appearing cumbersome and labor intensive at initial glance, item analysis is not a complex activity. One must keep in mind that item analysis will be applied only to those questions that need analysis or checks on their validity. Therefore, in most testing situations the process will be applied to probably only 5-10% of the questions. Item analysis allows one to check, on the basis of performance, the validity of questions, by determining if students who received the highest scores on the total test were successful in obtaining the correct answer on the questions being analyzed. Figure 8 shows a chart indicating how item analysis is performed.

Figure 8

Item Analysis Chart

Question No._____

Response	A	B	C	D	F
Correct					
Incorrect					

This chart shows the responses of students who received A's, B's, C's, or D's across the top of the chart. The left hand column shows which of the students achieved the correct answer for the question and which ones responded with the incorrect answer. In order to perform item analysis, one must record in the appropriate space the information for which the chart asks. That is, how many A students responded with the correct answer and how many responded incorrectly. This process is continued until all possible combinations are exhausted. Obviously, from this point on, individuals can become as statistically sophisticated as they wish. One can run correlations, percentages, etc. The bottom line, however, is simply to answer the question: Did students who received high percentage scores on the total test also respond in a similar percentage of correct answers on the question being analyzed and vice versa. Obviously, if the A students received 92% correct answers and above and only 50% correct responses on the question being analyzed it could be assumed it probably is not a valid question.

Item analysis is a simple technique quickly conducted and probably greatly under-utilized. It is a very simple process to get an indication of the validity of questionable test items and provides to faculty members the opportunity to reword or rephrase the questions so that they more accurately reflect the intent. As was indicated earlier the simple process described here is not intended to be statistically foolproof, however, it is certainly an improvement over the possibility of guessing concerning such validity or worse the possibility of leaving an invalid question or series of questions in an otherwise effective instrument.

SUMMARY

This chapter has attempted to review and provide some major criteria involved in the development of evaluation instruments, their validity and their resultant evaluation of students. All of the topics here, of course, can be discussed in significant detail in entire publications. It is the intent of this chapter to provide adjunct faculty with structure in which to develop a valid and reliable evaluation system utilizing professional techniques and expertise.

REFERENCES

1. Bloom, B.S., *et al., Taxonomy of Educational Objectives,* New York: David McKay Co., 1956.
2. Greive, Donald, *et al., Teaching in College: A Resource for Adjunct and Part-Time Faculty,* Cleveland: Info-Tec, Inc., 1983.
3. Mager, Robert F., *Preparing Instructional Objectives,* Belmont, Calif.: Fearon Publishers, 1962.